Travel Through Time
Cycle Power

Two-wheeled Travel Past and Present

Jane Shuter

Raintree

www.raintreepublishers.co.uk
Visit our website to find out more information about **Raintree** books.

To order:

 Phone 44 (0) 1865 888112

 Send a fax to 44 (0) 1865 314091

Visit the Raintree Bookshop at **www.raintreepublishers.co.uk** to browse our catalogue and order online.

First published in Great Britain by Raintree, Halley Court, Jordan Hill, Oxford OX2 8EJ, part of Harcourt Education.
Raintree is a registered trademark of Harcourt Education Ltd.

Editorial: Nick Hunter and Catherine Clarke
Design: Michelle Lisseter and bigtop
Picture Research: Maria Joannou and Kathryn Kollberg
Production: Jonathan Smith

Originated by Dot Gradations Ltd
Printed and bound in China by South China Printing Company

ISBN 1 844 43506 7
08 07 06 05 04
10 9 8 7 6 5 4 3 2 1

British Library Cataloguing in Publication Data
Shuter, Jane
Cycle Power: two wheeled travel past and present.
– (Travel Through Time)
388.3'47'09
A full catalogue record for this book is available from the British Library.

Acknowledgements
The publishers would like to thank the following for permission to reproduce photographs: Advertising Archives p. **21**; ATM Images pp. **18**, **28**; Bicycle Bill p. **9**; Harcourt Education pp. **4**, **12**; Henry Ford Museum and Greenfield Village p. **10**; Hulton Archive pp. **7**, **11**, **13**, **14**, **15**; Magnum Pictures p. **20**; Mary Evans Picture Library p. **6**; Photodisc p. **23**; Popperfoto pp. **8**, **16**, **17**, **24**, **29**; Robert Harding Picture Library (Gavin Hellier) p. **5**; Science Photo Library (Mark Clarke) p. **26**; Sporting Pictures p. **22**; Steven Behr p. **25**; Topham Picturepoint p. **19**; Trevor Clifford p. **27**.

Cover photograph of a bicycle poster from the 1860s reproduced with permission of Advertising Archives.

Every effort has been made to contact copyright holders of any material reproduced in this book. Any omissions will be rectified in subsequent printings if notice is given to the publishers.

The paper used to print this book comes from sustainable resources.

Contents

Any words appearing in bold, **like this**, are explained in the Glossary.

Travel on two wheels

The earliest people walked everywhere. People were glad to find faster, less tiring, ways of getting around. First, they rode animals, usually horses, donkeys or mules. Horses cost a lot to buy, feed and shelter. Only the **wealthy** had horses to ride. In desert places some people used camels.

Later, people began to travel by **vehicle**. The first vehicles were carts, pulled by animals. Vehicles with four wheels needed tracks and roads to move on.

In ancient times, poor people walked. Wealthy people rode, or were carried by people in chairs with handles.

A great invention?

The first bicycle was **invented** in 1817. People could ride bikes easily in places that carts or **coaches** could not go. Bikes were not very comfortable and it was not easy to take a passenger, but they were cheap and easy to run. They have been popular ever since.

WHAT IS A BIKE?

'Bike' is short for 'bicycle'. The word comes from Latin, which is an ancient language. In Latin 'bi' means 'two' and 'cycle' means 'wheel'. So a bicycle is a vehicle with two wheels.

As well as bikes, there is also a tricycle in this photo. 'Tri' means 'three' in Latin.

Early bikes

The first bike was **invented** in Germany in 1817. It had no **gears**, pedals or brakes. It was called the 'running machine' because the rider sat on the saddle and moved by running with big strides! A fit rider could, after much practice, go up to 14 kilometres (9 miles) per hour.

KIRKPATRICK MACMILLAN

Kirkpatrick Macmillan invented the first pedal bike in 1839. Macmillan, a Scottish blacksmith, made several bikes. They worked well but never became well known or popular. Macmillan did not share his ideas.

These men are riding 'running machines'. The man in the background is taking very long strides.

The velocipede

The next bike to arrive was built in France in 1861. It was built by Pierre Michaux and was called the velocipede. As yet, no one had called a bike a bike! The velocipede was very popular. By 1865 the family were selling 400 bikes a year. In 1871 a new bike, the 'ordinary', also called the **penny-farthing**, was invented. It had a large wheel at the front and a small wheel at the back. The wheel at the front travelled a long way each time it turned.

The penny-farthing bike was hard to get on to but it didn't stop people racing on them!

Bone shakers

In the 1880s, bike wheels were made the same size as each other. These bikes had a brake, as had some **penny-farthings**.

Before the 1880s, bikes were made with different-sized wheels. The wood and metal would have been very uncomfortable.

A better ride?

The new **design** of bike was easier to get on and off. Its brakes were better, but it was very uncomfortable. The hard rubber tyres meant that every bump shook the frame and rider – it was nicknamed the 'bone shaker'. It had no **gears**, so was hard to control. Gears help you to control a bike by changing the amount the wheels go around for each turn of the pedal.

Even though they were uncomfortable, bikes were popular. They were far cheaper than cars, and easier to manage. On a bike, a person could go much further than on foot.

BUILDING BETTER BIKES

Here are some early steps to building better bikes:

1817   two wooden wheels, no pedals, brakes or gears
1839   pedals, but no brakes or gears
1871   pedals, brakes, metal rimmed wheels, but no gears
1874   pedals, brakes, same size wheels, but no gears.

Adults only

In the 1880s there were no bikes for young children. Even the smallest bike needed long teenage or adult legs to reach the pedals.

By the late 1800s, bikes were being made with both wheels the same size.

Tricycles and tandems

Each extra set of pedals on a bike makes it longer and more wobbly!

Bikes have two wheels. Some bike makers thought three-wheeled cycles would be more popular. They were certainly more stable and easier to ride.

It soon became clear that two wheels worked best. Bicycles were the fastest – an ordinary person could cycle at about 24 kilometres (15 miles) per hour. Tricycle riders only travelled at about 11 kilometres (7 miles) per hour. Bikes could move around more easily and took up less space on the road.

A bicycle made for two?

Bikes for more than one person were also tried out.
At first, in the 1880s, bike makers made **tandems** – bikes
for two people.

LESS PRACTICAL?

Tricycles were not as wobbly to ride as bicycles. Women were less likely to get their long skirts tangled in the wheels. Tricycles were less useful in heavy traffic, though, because they were almost as wide as a **coach** or cart.

It would have been much easier to ride through this traffic on a bicycle than on a tricycle.

Women on wheels

Early cyclists were mostly men, partly because of the way people thought about women in the 1860s. For example, a woman on a bike might show her legs, which was seen as very rude.

In the USA there were schools where men and women learned to ride bikes.

Problem clothes

Clothes made cycling a problem for women in the 1800s. They wore several layers of skirts down to the ground, which easily tangled in bike wheels. Many of them wore tight underwear, called **corsets**, which made it hard to breathe too deeply.

Women wanted to cycle, no matter what the problems. Some used tricycles, which could be ridden sitting in a seat. Others wore special 'biking' clothes. Most popular were **knickerbockers** – baggy trousers fastened just below the knee. As more and more women rode bikes people got used to lady bikers.

BIKES FOR WOMEN

From 1895 bike makers began to make bikes just for women. These bikes had a guard to stop skirts catching. They were a big success.

These women are wearing long skirts, but their bikes have cycle guards.

Safety bikes

In 1885 the first 'safety-bike' was made. It had two equal-sized wheels joined by a chain that was also joined to the pedals. The wheels were smaller than earlier wheels, so the bike wobbled less. The chain controlled both wheels and made it easier to steer.

A more comfortable ride

In 1888 J. B. Dunlop re-**invented** the air-filled tyre. These had first been invented for use on **coach** wheels in the 1840s, but the coach weight burst the tyres too often. They worked better on bikes, which were lighter.

This photograph shows J.B.Dunlop's son on the first bike with air-filled tyres, in 1888.

The Tour de France is 2428 kilometres (1510 miles) long.

THE TOUR DE FRANCE

Bike racing became a sport in the 1900s. The first Tour de France bike race in 1903 was a big success. The next year everyone wanted to win. Lots of racers cheated. Some paid people to block the road with trees or carts!

From about 1890, bike makers began to make different bikes for different people, including ladies and children. In 1877 **gears** were used for the first time. Gears change the number of times the wheels go round for each turn of the pedal. They make the bikes more controllable and riding up hills easier.

Early motorbikes

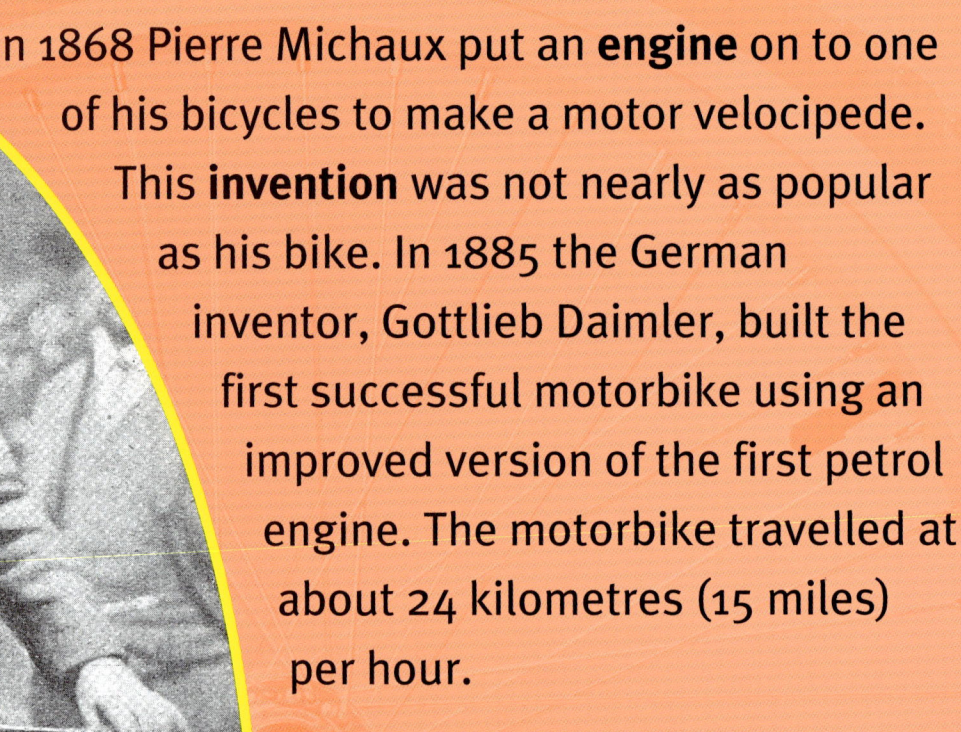

In 1868 Pierre Michaux put an **engine** on to one of his bicycles to make a motor velocipede. This **invention** was not nearly as popular as his bike. In 1885 the German inventor, Gottlieb Daimler, built the first successful motorbike using an improved version of the first petrol engine. The motorbike travelled at about 24 kilometres (15 miles) per hour.

Far from comfortable

Daimler's motorbike had a wooden frame and the wooden wheels had iron bands around them to move more easily over the road and make them wear more slowly. It was very bumpy for the rider.

Daimler's motorbike had a wood and iron frame, just like bikes at the time.

PROBLEMS OF EARLY MOTORBIKES

Early motorbikes threw up a lot of dust or mud from the roads. A rider going at full speed got cold, as well as dirty. Because cars and motorbikes were new inventions, there were not many garages and owners had trouble finding petrol. They usually had to do their own repairs, too.

This motorcyclist, dressed for the rainy day, would have found it hard to see **pedestrians** or other traffic.

In 1903 the US motorbike makers Harley-Davidson made their first all metal motorbike. It was designed as a racing bike and could reach speeds of up to 72 kilometres (45 miles) per hour.

Scooters

Scooters, first made in 1947, had small **engines**. They were faster than bikes, but slower than motorbikes. They were smaller and easier to ride than motorbikes. They could 'scoot' through traffic and the engine was strong enough to get them up steep hills.

Scooters came in many bright colours.

Italian style

Lambretta, in Italy, was one of the first companies to make scooters. It gave them a very different style from motorbikes. Scooters came in 'pretty' colours as well as ordinary ones, to appeal to women.

Scooters worked best in cities and towns. Scooter riders avoided traffic jams by weaving in and out of them, although this could be very dangerous. Scooters were not good on bumpy, unpaved roads and they were not fast enough to cover long distances. So they never became popular in big countries, such as the USA or Australia, where long distance travel was important.

IMAGE MAKING

What made scooters fashionable? By the 1950s adverts and films made the things in them popular. People copied film star fashions. It made scooters fashionable.

Scooters were used in the film *Roman Holiday*. This advert for the film shows three of its stars with a scooter.

Bikes and lifestyles

From the 1950s onwards bike companies built different motorbikes for different kinds of customers. People bought the motorbike that fitted in with the lifestyle they had – or wanted to have.

Some companies concentrated on making faster bikes, others on making bikes that looked different.

MODS AND ROCKERS

In 1960s Britain two sorts of 'biker look' were popular. 'Rockers' drove motorbikes. They wore scruffy leather jackets, had tattoos and listened to rock music. 'Mods' drove **scooters**. They wore neat suits and sunglasses.

In the 1960s 'chopper' motorbikes were very popular.

The most widespread idea of the motorbike rider was a young, cool **rebel**. Bike makers noticed how popular motorbikes were. In the late 1960s they made bikes that copied the motorbike look, with high handles and thicker wheels.

Kids who were too young to ride motorbikes wanted chopper bikes like this, which copied the motorbike look.

SPEEDING UP

Some motorbike makers concentrated on making a faster motorbike. These are the fastest speeds, as given by the makers:

1868 30 kilometres (19 miles) an hour
1912 72 kilometres (45 miles) an hour
1955 97 kilometres (60 miles) an hour
2000 282 kilometres (175 miles) an hour.

Racing bikes

Bikes and motorbikes are mainly used for travelling. They are also used for sport, for racing on special tracks or courses. Riders go as fast as possible and do not have to worry about traffic.

Motorcycle racing

Motorbikes race on special courses over fields or on flat, sandy tracks. Outdoor motorbike racing is noisy, as the **engines** whine at top speed. It is dirty, too. Riders get very hot and dusty in summer and muddy and wet in winter.

These racers are racing on ice. They need to have very good balance.

Indoor bike racing is clean and quiet. In competitions, often all you can hear is the hiss of the tyres on the track. Modern Olympic bikes use new materials to make the fastest bikes. Strengthened plastic and titanium steel are both light and strong and are used to replace metal parts.

FASTER BIKES

These are the fastest speeds for ordinary bikes in different years:

1817 14 kilometres (9 miles) an hour
1839 23 kilometres (14 miles) an hour
1885 31 kilometres (19 miles) an hour
1990 48 kilometres (30 miles) an hour.

The handles on a racing bike are low. The biker crouches over the front wheel for more speed.

Mountain bikes

Mountain bikes are a late 20th century **invention**. The first mountain bike was invented in the USA in 1979. The inventors, Gary Fisher and Charles Kelly, wanted to make a bike that could cope with tracks and steep hills easily.

Just more gears?

Mountain bikes have more **gears** to cope with steep hills. They also need light frames and thick tyres. The handlebars need to be the right shape so that a rider can change gear quickly and easily. All the parts need to be very strong.

In 1998, this engineer invented the world's lightest foldable bike. These bikes are very useful for people in big cities.

These racers have to wear cycle helmets. Many ordinary bikers do, too.

Mountain bikes quickly became very popular. People saw them as a way of getting fit. They used bikes to get to work in town, because they moved well through traffic. They could also use it to get away in their time off, as they could ride it over all sorts of bumpy ground and up and down steep hills.

BITS AND PIECES

Modern bikers need:
- a helmet
- proper lights to be seen at night
- a lock, to keep the bike safe when they leave it
- a repair kit.

Biking now

Modern biking has become difficult and dangerous, as road traffic has grown. Bikers in towns often have to deal with heavy traffic. They have to obey the same road rules as drivers of other **vehicles**. They breathe in air that is heavily **polluted** by petrol **fumes**.

Bike lanes

In some towns and cities there are bike lanes marked on the road or pavement. Only bikes can use them. Some places have special 'bike routes' marked, too. These show bikers how to get around without using busy main roads.

In big cities you might need to wear a face mask to protect yourself from pollution.

Modern bikes come in all shapes and sizes. There are cheap bikes with few **gears** and no equipment. There are expensive mountain bikes and all sorts of bikes in between. Bike makers are even making tricycles again.

There is now a huge range of bikes in all sizes to choose from.

KID'S PLAY

There are bikes and trikes for young people of all ages. First bikes often have two small wheels fixed to the back wheel. These are called **stabilizers** and help the rider to keep their balance. Safety helmets come in all sizes, too.

Into the future

Biking is good exercise and it does not cause **pollution**. Bikes are cheap to run. People who travel to work by bike do not have to pay bus or train fares or buy petrol. All of these things make biking seem a good way to travel, especially over shorter distances.

Motorbike companies are making motorbikes that are cheaper to run and do not cause as much pollution as cars. They hope more people will use motorbikes for their daily travel.

Some modern motorbikes have been re-**designed** to be more comfortable and to save petrol.

Traffic and pollution are getting worse in towns and cities. Some places are banning traffic in some areas. In 2003 London, UK, introduced a charge for driving in the centre of the city during the week. Sales of motorbikes, bikes and **scooters** went up.

Bikes can carry loads that would be too awkward for a person to carry.

Find out for yourself

You can find out more about the history of bikes by talking to older people about how travel has changed during their lifetimes. Your local library will have books about the subject. They may have newspapers and magazine articles, as well.

You will find the answers to many of your questions in this book, but you can also use other books and the Internet.

Books to read

Designed for Success: Superbikes, Ian Graham (Heinemann Library, 2003)
Extreme Sports: Mountain Biking, Ian Osborne (Raintree, 2003)
Take Off!: Transport Around the World: Motorbikes, Chris Oxlade (Heinemann Library, 2001)

Using the Internet

Explore the Internet to find out more about two-wheeled travel. Websites can change, but if the link below no longer works, don't worry. Use a search engine, such as www.yahooligans.com or www.internet4kids.com, and type in keywords such as '**penny-farthing**', 'Tour de France', '**scooter**' and 'Harley-Davidson'.

Websites

http://www.pedalinghistory.com
Visit the New York Pedaling History Museum website and find out more about the museum's collection of bikes and the history of the bicycle.

Disclaimer
All the Internet addresses (URLs) given in this book were valid at the time of going to press. However, due to the dynamic nature of the Internet, some addresses may have changed, or sites may have ceased to exist since publication. While the author and publishers regret any inconvenience this may cause readers, no responsibility for any such changes can be accepted by either the author or the publishers.

Glossary

coach four-wheeled vehicles for road travel, pulled by horses

corset underwear that is laced up to pull the waist in to look small

design plan or way of making something to do a certain job

engine piece of machinery that uses fuel to power something

fumes smelly, often poisonous, gasses given off by something. Traffic fumes are given off by petrol.

gears device used to control a bike by changing the number of times the wheels go round on each turn of the pedal. Faster turning helps to go uphill.

invent to make or discover something for the first time

knickerbockers loose trousers that are buttoned just below the knee

pedestrian person walking from one place to another

penny-farthing another name for the 'ordinary' bike which had a big wheel at the front and a small one at the back. The name comes from two coins that were used in the UK at the time. The penny was much bigger than the farthing, so the wheels looked like a penny and a farthing side by side.

pollution making something dirty, messy, often unsafe

rebel person who behaves differently than most people

scooter simple motorbike with a small engine

stabilizers small wheels that fit on to the back wheel of a bike, helping a rider to balance

tandem bike that is ridden by two people

vehicle something that is used to move around in

wealthy well off. Wealthy people have a lot of money to spend.

Index

Titles in the *Travel Through Time* series include:

Hardback   1 844 43506 7

Hardback   1 844 43502 4

Hardback   1 844 43503 2

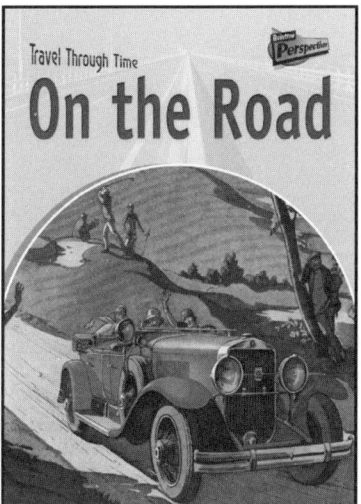

Hardback   1 844 43504 0

Hardback   1 844 43505 9

Hardback   1 844 43507 5

Find out about the other titles in this series on our website www.raintreepublishers.co.uk